D1714057

# *Jesus is Better:*

*Idolatry, Struggle, and the Challenge of Being a Teenager in a Disenchanted World*

by

**Lucas Shipman**

This book is dedicated to:

The Children at Happy Hill Farm

Your hopefulness in the midst of difficult life situations inspires us all. My work with each and every one of you has changed my life. Keep walking by faith and build your life upon the only solid rock, Jesus Christ!

# Table of Contents

# Acknowledgements

First, I want to thank my beautiful wife, Natalie, for inspiring me and sticking by my side through many seasons of ministry. Her daily prayers for me have been used by the Lord to bear much fruit in our life -- including the creation of this book. This devotional is a direct result of many years of ministry to the youth at Happy Hill Farm. Without my grandparents, Ed and Gloria, responding to the Lord's call on their life to start a home for children; and my parents, Chuck and Janie; uncle and aunt, Todd and Linda; sister and brother-in-law, Amanda and Steven; and all the wonderful staff at HHF continuing that work -- none of this would be possible. I also want to thank Paul Gould for his mentorship and encouragement during and after my seminary education. I appreciate your personal recommendation of this devotional and your friendship. Travis McNeely, thank you for your topic suggestions and early feedback on this book. I am thankful for our friendship and the hospitality we always receive from Woodlawn Baptist Church. The elders at Grace Church Southwest have had a profound impact on my life, and the lives of my family, over these last few years: Matt Weaver, Rick Driggers, and Ryan Keeney - you are a beloved "band of brothers!" Special thanks to Chris Lee for his research, work on the manuscript, and editing. I also acknowledge Chris Taft's work on the manuscript and his daily work for Happy Hill Farm! To my children -- Max, Piper, and Graham, I pray you will live a joyful life of trusting in Christ alone. I love you, and Jesus loves you fuller and deeper than I ever can. Run to Him. Finally, my uncle, Todd Shipman, helped tremendously in editing. Thank you!

## Introduction for Families and Leaders

**The greatest enemy to a teenager's soul is not outside them, but *inside them.***

Sinful desires and idolatry give birth to death. At the end of the journey of following Jesus is eternal joy in his presence -- at the end of the journey worshiping idols is eternal death.

Christian parents, grandparents, Sunday school teachers, and student pastors often share a common goal. They want the children under their care to go out into the world with a Christian Worldview, but worldview training is often centered on "apologetics," the defense of the Christian faith. I support teaching teenagers the logical and evidential reasons for our faith. We *should* teach our teenagers why naturalism is a faulty way to view the universe. We *should* teach our kids that the Bible is not, in fact, anti-woman or pro-slavery. We *should* teach our kids the reasons why we can trust the 66 books of the Bible, the historical evidence for the resurrection of Jesus, and the overwhelming proof our universe was designed. These topics should come up in every home, youth group, and Christian school. **However, apologetics training is not enough for teenagers. Developing a Christian Worldview involves more than apologetics.**

Your kids are not being "argued" out of the church by anti-Christian philosophers. Their hearts are being captured by other stories and desires. **Simply put, they are being influenced and persuaded to worship idols instead of Jesus.** That is why we are seeing youth leave the church in record numbers.[1]

This devotional is not a worldview or apologetics curriculum. Its intention is to address some of the most common idols young people struggle with daily.

I want to help you prepare their hearts for whatever occurs in their lives. I want this devotional, with its daily questions and Biblical readings, to inspire real conversations to take place. My hope is the Gospel will speak to their hearts, sins will be confessed and repented of, and their newfound faith will lead to improved lives.

My family and I help kids overcome their past circumstances to become all that God created them to be. We've done this important work on a beautiful, 500-acre Christian boarding school campus, right outside of the DFW metroplex, for almost 50 years. I've been a pastor, youth leader, teacher, and "discipler" of teenagers for a large part of my adult life. I'm excited to go on this journey with you to identify and eliminate, with God's help, some "idols" in your teenager's heart.

**Some of the best work done in the world of Christian apologetics include the CSB Apologetics Study Bible for Students and books by William Lane Craig, Paul Gould, Sean McDowell,

---

[1] LifeWay Research, 2019 https://lifewayresearch.com/2019/01/15/most-teenagers-drop-out-of-church-as-young-adults/.

and J. P. Moreland. Check them out and give copies to your kids or students.**

# Introduction for Students

**What is an idol?**  Most people envision a statue made of stone or gold, and they have a picture in their mind with ancient people bowing down before it.  While there have been these kinds of idols in the past, the word "idol" encompasses a great deal more.

In today's world, many people might think that the word "idol" is a positive thing, as in the TV show, "American Idol".  Talented young people all working hard to become famous for their singing ability.  In fact, many of the things we might "idolize" can be good things that God has provided -- fame, money, or power -- if they are viewed as gifts from God to be used for the good of others.  A famous and rich person with power can use his or her wealth and position to help others, to bring important issues to light, and to build up a community for the good of everyone.  When a gift from God becomes an "idol," it is because we raise its importance above God.  It takes priority in our life.  When we are happy or sad, instead of going toward God, we move toward the things we have placed above Him and turned into idols.  We sacrifice our time and energy for them.  We give our emotions over to them and their pursuit.  We try to find fulfillment in them.  They become a large part of our identity.

Humans were created to worship God, and striving to fill that need with other things -- money, sex, popularity, religion, physical fitness and appearance, entertainment -- will leave a hole in your heart that can never be satisfied.

The Bible has many warnings about greed and the most common idols related to it. Greed fuels the worship of many idols:

**1 Timothy 6:10**
For the love of money is a root of all kinds of evil.[2]

**Colossians 3:5**
Put to death, therefore, whatever belongs to your earthly nature: sexual immorality, impurity, lust, evil desires, and greed, which is idolatry.[3]

**Proverbs 15:27**
The greedy bring ruin to their households....[4]

**Proverbs 28:25**
The greedy stir up conflict, but those who trust in the LORD will prosper.[5]

**1 Corinthians 10:14[6]**
Therefore, my dear friends, flee from idolatry.

When you desire something more than God, it can quickly become an idol in your life.  Unlike God, your Creator, idols are not

---

[2] 1 Tim. 6:10 (NIV).
[3] Col. 3:5 (NIV).
[4] Prov. 15:27 (NIV).
[5] Prov. 28:25 (NIV).
[6] 1 Cor. 10:14 (NIV).

perfect. They will not be forever faithful to you. They won't last forever. And they will not satisfy you. There will always be:

More money and things to strive after;
A better friend to be found;
A greater athletic achievement;
A more perfect partner;
A better job;
A higher "high;" or
Another 1000 "followers."

**Isaiah 44:9**

All who make idols are nothing, and the things they treasure are worthless. Those who would speak up for them are blind; they are ignorant, to their own shame.[7]

As we examine some of the more common things that people turn into idols, my hope is that you will come to understand at a young age that only your relationship with Jesus can provide true contentment and lead to eternal salvation. As you go through life, you will worship something. If not God, then you will constantly strive to find happiness in temporary things that turn into idols in your life. God wants you to have strong desires. He just wants them to be directed toward Him!

---

[7] Isaiah 44:9 (NIV).

**C.S. Lewis,** in his book, **The Weight of Glory, and Other Addresses**, says:

> "It would seem that Our Lord finds our desires not too strong, but too weak. We are half-hearted creatures, fooling about with drink and sex and ambition when infinite joy is offered us, like an ignorant child who wants to go on making mud pies in a slum because he cannot imagine what is meant by the offer of a holiday at the sea. We are far too easily pleased."

Meaningless idols can accept your time, talents, desires, and hard work as you look for fulfillment in them that will never come. It is because these idols can never give anything back to you. There can be no two way relationship, as you can have with your Creator.

### Hebrews 4:14-16

Therefore, since we have a great high priest who has ascended into heaven, Jesus the Son of God, let us hold firmly to the faith we profess.

For we do not have a high priest who is unable to empathize with our weaknesses, but we have one who has been tempted in every way, just as we are--yet he did not sin.

Let us then approach God's throne of grace with confidence, so that we may receive mercy and find grace to help us in our time of need.[8]

Remember that God is faithful and forever. He is perfect, and His plan for your life is as well.

**There are no second-generation Christians. God has no grand-children**. The faith of your parents, grandparents, or mentors is not enough to save you. No one is "in" by default. Everyone is born into sin and needs a savior. Each of us has to repent, believe, and be born again.

As you go out into the world, your faith must be your own. The greatest danger to your soul is not the negative influence of an atheist professor or friend. The greatest danger to your soul is found within yourself and your own sinful desires.

If you are not a Christian, I pray you meet Jesus during this study. If you are a Christian, it is easy in today's world to be drawn away from the things that really matter. You might forget what Christ has done for you, find yourself believing another "story," and shift your desires away from the Lord. This shift can wreck your life

Every one of us has worshipped idols in our lives. We may not have  bowed before a statue or sacrificed at a pagan altar, but

---

[8] Hebrews 4:14-16 (NIV).

we've done something worse. At times, we have sacrificed our relationships with people, by focusing on our own selfish desires.

When Jesus saves you, He starts a lifelong process of walking with you and helping you to grow in holiness. He will help you overcome the idols in your life. It might not be easy at times. Some of our idols have been given much time and attention, and even though we know they have never provided true happiness, they still have a hold on us. We think that the next thing we buy will make us happy. The next relationship will provide perfect bliss. The next "high" will fulfill us. Idols will never satisfy you. Jesus wants to set you free.

As we examine some of the idols to which we hold, think about how many times you have been disappointed in them, and do not go down the path of hoping a new idol might prove different.

Most of you would agree with this statement, "I am a sinner." However, knowing that fact is not enough to identify and destroy the idols that keep us from Jesus. They must be named, called out, and confessed, and when they are, I promise you Jesus' love will be better than any of those "idols."

# The Idol of Religious Accomplishment

Church attendance cannot save your soul. The faith of your parents or grandparents cannot save your soul. Bible verse memory, attending a church, and getting baptized cannot save your soul. Those are all wonderful things, but apart from Jesus, those are meaningless. Walking with other believers is essential to growing in faith, but you won't "catch" salvation from them by proximity. The Father calls, Jesus saves, and the Spirit makes us alive. It sounds simple, but Judas spent a lot of time around some special people, yet his idols came before his relationship with Jesus.

In Philippians 3:4-6, the apostle Paul says that no one has a more impressive religious heritage than him:

> *If anyone else thinks he has reason for confidence in the flesh, I have more:  circumcised on the eighth day, of the people of Israel, of the tribe of Benjamin, a Hebrew of Hebrews; as to the law, a Pharisee;  as to zeal, a persecutor of the church; as to righteousness under the law, blameless* (ESV).

He then calls his heritage rubbish. The Greek word he uses is even stronger than that. You've probably stepped in it if you've ever been to a farm.

Verses 7-11:

> *Indeed, I count **everything as loss** because of the surpassing worth of knowing Christ Jesus my Lord. For his sake I have suffered the loss of all things and count them as **rubbish**, in order that I may gain Christ and be found in him, not having a righteousness of my own that comes from the law, but that which comes through faith in Christ, the righteousness from God that depends on faith -- that I may know him and the power of his resurrection, and may share his sufferings, becoming like him in his death, that by any means possible I may attain the resurrection from the dead* (ESV).

Count whatever religious pedigree you come from as garbage compared to knowing Christ. Many confuse being religious with obeying Jesus. *You cannot earn your way to God. You do not deserve salvation.* The only way to be saved is by faith in Jesus' perfect work for you.

Charles Spurgeon said, "If your religion does not make you holy, it will damn you. It is simply painted pageantry to go to hell in." Thinking you are not as bad as Hitler does not satisfy the standard of holiness. Jesus is the standard of holiness. Some religions have a sliding scale of works, but Biblical Christianity says there is no holiness apart from Jesus. **Compare yourself to Scripture, not other Christians.** Christianity is not a new religion for you to try. Biblical Christianity is new birth! Good works come from a new heart that has been changed by God.

**Further Reading in Scripture:**

- John 3:1--21
- Philippians 3:4-6
- Colossians 2:23
- James 1:26

**Reflection**:

1. Do you believe you are "good with God" because you just try to be good? What does the Bible actually say about "new birth?" (It's required to be a part of the Kingdom of God.) Read John 3:1-21.

2. Ephesians 2:8-9 says, *"For you are saved by grace through faith, and this is not from yourselves; it is God's gift--not from works so that no one can boast."* The Bible clearly teaches that those who trust in themselves (their good works, their family's faith, or their church attendance) are **not** saved. Only those who trust in Christ alone for their salvation **are saved**. Discuss this.

3. Have you personally turned from your sins and trusted (believed) that only Jesus can save you because of His sacrifice on the cross? Acts 3:19-20 says, *"Therefore repent and turn back, so that your sins may be wiped out, that seasons of refreshing may come from the presence of the Lord, and that he may send Jesus, who has been appointed for you as the Messiah (anointed King over all)."*

**Further Readings:**

- Ferguson, Sinclair. *The Whole Christ: Legalism, Antinomianism, and Gospel Assurance.* Wheaton, IL: Crossway, 2016.
- Greear, J. D. *Gospel: Recovering the Power that Made Christianity Revolutionary.* Nashville, TN: B & H Books, 2011.
- Vickers, Brian. *Justification by Grace Through Faith: Finding Freedom from Legalism, Lawlessness, Pride, and Despair.* Phillipsburg, NJ: P&R Publishing Co., 2013.
- Washer, Paul. *The Gospel Call and True Conversion.* Grand Rapids, MI: Reformation Heritage Books, 2013.

# The Idol of Gender Identity

Some of you find your identity in your uniqueness: "I like these things;" "I'm good at this, and that makes me unique;" "I'm different," etc. You may even believe that your gender identity makes you unique, and it defines who you are.

Sam Allberry has powerful insight:

> [Jesus'] love entirely reshapes how we see ourselves...we tend to find our identity in who we love most. It is why sexuality has such a powerful effect on our identity. The sort of attractions we experience, and the sort of people we feel attracted to, easily form a key (or the key) to who we understand ourselves to be. Sexual identity has become a powerful force in Western society.[9]

He continues:

> We have made sexuality the foundation to self-understanding. Sexual behavior has therefore become a primary means of self-expression. To

---

[9]Alberry, Sam. *Why Does God Care Who I Sleep with?* (Oxford: The Good Book Company, 2020), 102.

restrict sexual behavior is to stop someone from being who they are.[10]

Both homosexuality and transsexuality are dangers to the human soul. The percentage of U.S. adults who identify as LGBTQ+ has doubled over the past decade, from 3.5% in 2012 to 7.1% in 2021. People who identify as LGBTQ+ could make up 10 to 15% of the adult population "in the not too distant future" as Gen Z and millennials comprise an increasing share of the adult population, says Jeff Jones, the author of the Gallup poll to Axios.[11]

I am not here to deny the legitimate feelings and attractions of LGBTQ+ identifying people. Let's focus on gender "identity," since it is in the news every day.  Gender dysphoria is real and heartbreaking.

"This sense of a mismatch between physical sex and psychological gender is called gender dysphoria … they *deny* that gender identity is rooted in biology. Their argument is that gender is completely independent of the body."[12]

> "The implication is that *the body does not matter*. It is not the site of the authentic self. Matter does not matter. All that matters is a person's inner feelings or sense of self … if the meaning of our

---

[10]Ibid.
[11]Jones, Jeff *Gallup poll* (Gallup, 2022).
[12]Pearcey, Nancy *Love Thy Body,* 30-31.

sexuality is not something we derive *from* the body, then it becomes something we impose *on* the body."[13]

Condemnation, shame, and name-calling are antithetical to how the New Testament tells us to engage those in sin.

> *But in your hearts regard Christ the Lord as holy, ready at any time to give a defense to anyone who asks you for a reason for the hope that is in you.* **Yet do this with gentleness and reverence, keeping a clear conscience**, *so that when you are accused, those who disparage your good conduct in Christ will be put to shame. For it is better to suffer for doing good if that should be God's will, than for doing evil* (1 Peter 3:15-17 CSB).

How can those who suffer from gender dysphoria find freedom from that false god and idol?

> "Christianity assigns the human body a much richer dignity and value. Humans do not need freedom from the body to discover their true, authentic selves. **Rather we can celebrate our embodied existence as a good gift from God.**

---

[13]Ibid.

**Instead of escaping from the body, the goal is to live in harmony with it."**[14]

Humans are embodied souls. To try and separate the two in regards to sexuality and gender breaks away from the good reality that God created. It is to live in a world where the feelings of the individual dictate reality, not where God dictates reality. Calling transsexuality what it is -- gender dysphoria -- is a good thing. As with any idol in this book, this may be wrapped around your identity. The thought of abandoning this way of seeing the world and living in it might terrify you. I invite you to read a story from a Christian who struggled with that as well: *Gay Girl, Good God,* by Jackie Hill Perry.

**Further Reading in Scripture:**
- Genesis 1:26-27
- Romans 1:26-27
- 1 Corinthians 6:9-20
- 1 Thessalonians 4:1-8

**Reflection:**
1. Do you feel as though you are ruled by your sexual feelings?
2. Read 1 Corinthians 6:9-20.
3. Discuss the reality of elevated percentages of depression/anxiety and suicide amongst LGBTQ+

[14]Pearcey, Nancy *Love Thy Body.*

identifying individuals. Can you attribute these highly elevated numbers solely to cultural shame and pressure? Or might there be a spiritual weight to that lifestyle?

**Further Readings:**

- Allberry, Sam. *Is God Anti-gay?: And other questions about Homosexuality, the Bible, and Same-Sex Attraction.* Charlotte, NC: The Good Book Company, 2015.
- Comer, John Mark. *Live No Lies: Recognize and Resist the Three Enemies that Sabotage Your Peace.* Colorado Springs, CO: WaterBrook, 2021.
- Pearcey, Nancy. *Love Thy Body: Answering Hard Questions about Life and Sexuality.* Grand Rapids, MI: Baker Books, 2018.
- Sprinkle, Preston. *Embodied: Transgender Identities, The Church, and What the Bible Has to Say.* Colorado Springs, CO: David C. Cook, 2021.
- Yarhouse, Mark A. *Emerging Gender Identities: Understanding the Diverse Experiences of Today's Youth.* Grand Rapids, MI: Brazos Press, 2020.
- _____. *Understanding Gender Dysphoria: Navigating Transgender Issues in a Changing Culture.* Downers Grove, IL: InterVarsity Press, 2015.

# The Idol of Worldly Accomplishments

Some of you find your identity in what you do:

I am an actor. It's WHO I AM.

I am an athlete. It's WHO I AM.

I am a scientist. It's WHO I AM.

I am a musician. It's WHO I AM.

This is a dangerous belief system. Does your value change in God's eyes according to your accomplishments? Does He love you more or less?

You could get into a car accident and become wheelchair-bound. You could get injured during a game, and your whole athletic career could be over. You could have a stroke tonight and have your cognitive functions impaired forever.

Some of you find your identity in how "good" you are. You show up to church. You obey your parents. You've never been drunk or smoked weed. But what happens when you screw up?

Some of you find your identity in your family. Your grandma has never missed a church service. You are a good, solid family. Your family is successful. What happens when that changes?

At any moment, you could become physically or mentally disabled, or your family could fall apart. What then? Who are you then? Are you any less human? The answer is, no. Your worth is not tied to your abilities, what you accomplish, or from where you come. The idea that some human beings are worth more than others gave rise to slavery, the Holocaust, modern eugenics, and abortion "rights."

Every human being, from womb to tomb, is valuable because they are made in the image of God -- "unwanted" or "planned," average or below average, able or handicapped, young or old, male or female, and no matter the skin color or family background.

*Genesis 1:26-27:*

> *Then God said, "Let us make man in our image, according to our likeness. They will rule the fish of the sea, the birds of the sky, the livestock, the whole earth, and the creatures that crawl on the earth."*

> *So God created man*
> *in his own image;*
> *he created him in the image of God;*
> *he created them male and female.*

Without this foundation, who decides which humans have value. In the 1930s, Nazis said Jewish lives had no value. Today's Chinese government says Uyghur lives have no value. Modern western culture claims humans in their mother's wombs have no value.

All human life has value, not because of what the individual accomplishes or where they are from, but because their Creator, God, says so.

**Further Reading in Scripture**:
- Matthew 19:21
- 2 Corinthians 12:9
- Galatians 1:10
- Revelation 5 (see description of those around the throne in worship)

**Reflection**:
1. Do you find your identity in what you do? Or where (family/race/nation) you are from?
2. Have you ever thought negatively about a person just because of where they are from?
3. Read and Discuss: https://www.desiringgod.org/interviews/what-does-it-mean-to-be-made-in-gods-image.

**Further Readings**:
- Horton, Michael. *Ordinary: Sustainable Faith in a Radical, Restless World*. Grand Rapids, MI: Zondervan, 2014.
- Keller, Timothy. *Every Good Endeavor: Connecting Your Work to God's Work*. New York, NY: Penguin Books, 2014.

- Pace, Scott. *Answering God's Calling: Finding, Following, and Fulfilling God's Will for Your Life.* Nashville, TN: B&H Academic, 2020.
- Platt, David. *Radical: Taking Back Your Faith from the American Dream.* Colorado Springs, CO: Multnomah Books, 2010.
- Tozer, A. W. *Success and the Christian: The Cost of Spiritual Maturity.* Camps Hills, PA: Wingspread, 2006.

# The Idol of Instant Gratification & Entitlement

Studies have shown a prime indicator of future success in children is their ability to delay gratification.[15] Stanford University conducted a now-famous experiment on children in 1972 with marshmallows:

*In this study, a child was offered a choice between one small but immediate reward, or two small rewards if they waited for a period of time. During this time, the researcher left the room for about 15 minutes and then returned. The reward was either a marshmallow or pretzel stick, depending on the child's preference. In follow-up studies, the researchers found that children who were able to wait longer for the preferred rewards tended to have better life outcomes, as measured by SAT scores, educational attainment, body mass index (BMI), and other life measures.[16]*

Hopefully, most of you are not being tempted by marshmallows -- but there is an idol hiding in plain sight that many of us worship… entitlement. The idol of entitlement and the inability to delay gratification go hand in hand, and it's not just children in the 1970s who struggle with this. Part of what makes portable devices so dangerous to our souls is that they provide *instant gratification.* A

---

[15]*Predicting adolescent cognitive and self-regulatory competencies from preschool delay of gratification: Identifying diagnostic conditions* (Developmental Psychology, 1990).
[16]Wikipedia, *https://en.wikipedia.org/wiki/Stanford_marshmallow_experiment.*

funny video, an interesting article, a new product to buy, or a new pornographic image -- are all instantly accessible with a tap.

We are being trained to demand everything instantly. My children can't wrap their heads around buying something from a paper catalog and having to wait 4-8 weeks for it to finally arrive. This was the norm, even during my childhood. They are spoiled by *free two-day* shipping on everything.

This immediate need for gratification goes beyond products and internet access. Consider how *fast* we demand friendships to develop and be useful for us. If it seems difficult or long, we bail. We use people and love things instead of following the Biblical way of life: loving people and using things.

Living in a society where technology has made things so immediate, many of us have become entitled people. Consider how we demand attention online. Consider how we expect others to abide by the "rules" but not us. Consider how we judge churches by the feelings they give us when we walk in the door. *Did someone greet me? How's the music quality? Did the preacher have to clear his throat too many times this week? Did this sermon immediately apply to my life pleasantly?* Consider how we expect things to always be working -- the quick anger many express at spotty cell connections or bad wi-fi.

The idol of entitlement is a giant statue for so many. It is self-worship at breakneck speed. *I expect the world to cater to my every need -- because I am at the center.*

The Bible speaks in very different terms. At the center of the universe is the Risen, victorious King Jesus -- not some mere human. The Bible is also filled with "farming" language. Not just because that is what ancient Hebrew people would understand, but also to correct our pace of life. Farming is hard and dull, filled with waiting, hoping that God sends rain and sun (but not too much), trusting in Him to complete the work you started. Such is the Christian life. So, slow down. Know that when the feeling of "I deserve this" swells up in your heart -- you are being led into idol worship. We deserve nothing from God. But yet, He has lavished so much common grace upon mankind. He makes the sun rise on the righteous and unrighteous. He has saved countless sinners like me, who can so easily fall into entitled self-worship.

Nancy Leigh DeMoss says in her book, *Choosing Gratitude,*

> The consequences of an ungrateful spirit are not as readily seen as, say, those of a contagious disease. But they are no less deadly. Western civilization has fallen prey to an epidemic of ingratitude. Like a poisonous vapor, this subtle sin is polluting our lives, our homes, our churches, and our culture.[17]

**Further Reading in Scripture:**
- Lamentations 3:25-26
- Mark 10:21
- 1 Corinthians 13:4
- Ephesians 4:2
- 1 Peter 4:10-11

**Reflection**:
1. When do you notice that you demand things instantly in your life?
2. Consider the second to last paragraph of this devotional again … are you at the center of your universe?
3. How can you live a "slower" paced life for God's glory and your eternal good?

**Further Reading:**
- Crabtree, Sam. *Practicing Thankfulness: Cultivating a Grateful Heart in All Circumstances*. Wheaton, IL: Crossway, 2021.
- Crowe, Dustin. *The Grumbler's Guide to Giving Thanks*. Chicago, IL: Moody Publishers, 2020.
- DeMoss, Nancy Leigh, *Choosing Gratitude*: Your Journey to Joy. Chicago, IL: Moody Publishers, 2011.
- Voskamp, Ann. *One Thousand Gifts: A Dare to Live Fully Right Where You Are*. Grand Rapids, MI: Zondervan, 2010.

---

[17]Demss, Nancy Leigh. *Choosing Gratitude: Your Journey to Joy.* (Chicago: Moody Publishers, 2011).

# The Idol of Electronic Devices

When we examine the biblical imagery of idolatry, we see many parallels to a slave/owner relationship (Galatians 4:8, Isaiah 44:9-20). The closest modern idol to this imagery might be people glued to their devices. You've seen it. You might even be guilty of it; couples at dinner looking down at screens, kids unable to "be bored," people communicating more on their phones than face to face. While it is funny, it is also sad that people today will text each other while living in the same house or sitting across the table from each other.  Our devices have a way of becoming all-consuming idols.

Your phone might feel like it's tethered to your body. Elon Musk (founder of Tesla and SpaceX) recently said that humans have already turned cyborg because "we are so well integrated with our phones and computers."[18] That is a scary reality. Your phone is not a neutral device. The most popular apps you and I use have been created for a purpose. The primary function is to make *you and I* the "product" that attracts advertisers. Everything we do online is tracked, categorized, and kept to further refine how companies can market to our every desire. My point is this -- technology forms us to believe the lie that we are at the center of the universe -- not Jesus. Believing the lie that everything is about us causes us to spend more, post more, and live more of our lives online. Screen time doubled among youth during 2020 due to the pandemic --

---

[18]Musk, Elon..

almost 8 hours a day on average.[19] Facebook had internal documents leaked that showed they know that Instagram is bad for teenagers' mental health … the photo app could affect girls' mental health on issues such as body image and self-esteem.[20]

Real idolatry is a slave/owner relationship. Does your phone own you? Are you in control of it, or is it in control of you? Paul implores us to only let Christ (the one who died to purchase us) be in control of us (Romans 8:15; Galatians 2:20).

> "We run away like conscientious little bugs, scared rabbits, dancing attendance on our machines, our slaves, our masters"--clicking, scrolling, tapping, liking, sharing . . . anything. "We think we want peace and silence and freedom and leisure, but deep down we know that this would be unendurable to us." In fact, "we want to complexify our lives. We don't have to; we want to. We want to be harried and hassled and busy. Unconsciously, we want the very thing about which we complain. For if we had leisure, we would look at ourselves and listen to our hearts and see the great gaping hole in our hearts and be terrified, because that hole is so big that nothing but God can fill it."[21]

[19](JAMA Pediatrics, 2020).
[20](WSJ, 2021).
[21]Reinke, Tony *12 Ways Your Phone Is Changing You.*

What a sad reality many of us find ourselves in. Cry out to the Lord, and ask Him to break you free from this slavery to devices.

**Further Reading in Scripture:**
- Leviticus 19:4
- Psalm 135:15-18
- Isaiah 44:9-20
- 1 Corinthians 10:14

**Reflection:**
1. All smartphones keep track of your screen time if you enable those built-in apps. Turn those on if you haven't already. Discuss your daily use.
2. When was the last time you have been totally undistracted and alone with God? Does that scare you?
3. Begin to catalog the number of times your device interrupts conversations, meals, movies, etc. Can you really say you give uninterrupted focus to anything?

**Further Reading:**
- Crouch, Andy. *The Tech-Wise Family: Everyday Steps for Putting Technology in Its Proper Place*. Grand Rapids, MI: Baker Books, 2017.
- Reinke, Tony. *12 Ways Your Phone Is Changing You*. Wheaton, IL: Crossway, 2017.
- _____. *Competing Spectacles: Treasuring Christ in the Media Age*. Wheaton, IL: Crossway, 2019.

- _____. *God, Technology, and the Christian Life.* Wheaton, IL: Crossway, 2022.
- Song, Felicia We. *Restless Devices: Recovering Personhood, Presence, and Place in the Digital Age.* Downers Grove, IL: IVP Academic, 2021.

# The Idol of Money

"Get the money, dollar, dollar bill y'all" -- Wu-Tang Clan, *C.R.E.A.M*

*For the parents reading this, C.R.E.A.M. is an acronym of "Cash Rules Everything Around Me" and is a song by the American hip hop group, Wu-Tang Clan.*

Quit worshiping money.

Some of the loudest voices that speak on Christian giving are also heretical voices. The church in the west over the last 50 years has, by and large, failed to teach properly on money.

We've let two goofy groups of people dominate the conversation about Christians and money. Do not let yourself fall into one of these false teachings.

1. The prosperity "gospel" preachers. Think Creflo Dollar, Joel Osteen -- preachers who incorrectly teach that physical possessions and material wealth are almost a guaranteed side effect of being a Christian.
2. The anti-wealth movement. **"Poor is holy."** These Christians believe that any kind of enterprise, business success, wealth building, or influence, is a de facto worship of money.

Both groups are incredibly misguided and unbiblical.

The prosperity "gospel" is heresy. To say to someone, you are poor because you don't have enough faith, or you're sick because you've spoken it into your life is disgusting and unbiblical. Jesus never promised His followers material wealth. Any material wealth we have is simply a blessing from the Father -- and it is a blessing we will have to give an account for how we used it. [22] I do not have the space here to properly dismantle the prosperity "gospel," but I will make three observations. One, Jesus, our example and Savior, was homeless and poor during His earthly ministry. "Jesus told him, 'Foxes have dens, and birds of the sky have nests, but the Son of Man has no place to lay his head.'" [23] Two, Jesus Himself, [24] and the rest of the New Testament, echo with the promise that Christians will endure suffering in this life. "In fact, all who want to live a godly life in Christ Jesus will be persecuted."[25] Third, God uses suffering in this world to make us more like Jesus (1 Peter 4:12-19), and all suffering is not connected to a lack of faith.

To respond to the second group -- those that believe that being "poor is holy" -- wealth is not inherently evil. The Bible does not say, "Money is the root of all evil." It says, "For the *love* of money is a root of all kinds of evil, and by craving it, some have wandered away from the faith and pierced themselves with many griefs."[26]

---

[22]2 Timothy 3:12 (ESV).
[23]2 Timothy 3:12 (ESV).
[24]2 Timothy 3:12 (ESV).
[25]2 Timothy 3:12 (ESV).

Wealth is not inherently evil. If you make over 32 thousand dollars a year as a household, you are in the top 1% in the world. Did you hear that?

If your parents make over 32 thousand dollars as a household per year, they are in the top 1% worldwide.

If your parents make over 88 thousand dollars a year as a household, they are in the top 25% of Americans and in the top .02% of the world!

Wealth is not inherently evil. Business skills, an enterprising spirit, and the desire to build wealth so you can help others is not evil. It is also not a secular pursuit.

There is no secular/sacred divide. What you do for work and what you do in church is not divided. Whatever you do, do it all for the glory of God!

You shouldn't see things like jobs, investments, and influence in the community as *secular*.

The paycheck every two weeks is a gift from God. The side hustle income is a gift from God. The business your parents or

---

[26] 1 Timothy 6:10 (Berean Study Bible).

grandparents put their blood, sweat, and tears into is a gift from God.

If more Christians thought about wealth-building and influence-building properly, the world would change for the better.

Cash is not the problem, your heart is.

"We minimize and compartmentalize certain aspects of life and choose to believe that God only cares about things like prayer, Bible reading, church attendance, and the token good deed from time to time. This is a lie we tell ourselves and a lie Satan is happy to perpetuate. The enemy wins when our money is distant from our walk with Jesus, because our hearts will remain equally distant as well, and our resources will be less effective in the mission God has given us."[27]

As you begin to work, see every paycheck as a gift from God. It all belongs to Him, and He will ask you on Judgment Day what you did as a *steward* of His resources. Start to think of yourself as a *steward* instead of an *owner*. Nothing belongs to you -- not even your life! If you believe that money is a gift, you won't worship it as a god. Save it -- don't love it. Spend it wisely -- don't blow it. Invest it -- but don't find your hope in it. Money cannot save your life, so don't live your life just trying to accumulate it. Don't make it an idol. Use it for good.

---

[27]Munson, Jamie.

**Further Reading in Scripture:**
- Matthew 18:23-35
- Mark 10:17-30
- Colossians 3:5
- 1 Timothy 6:!0

**Reflection:**

1. Have you been living as a steward or an owner?
2. Have you seen anyone in your family worship money as a god? How has that gone for them?
3. Discuss the last paragraph in today's devotional.

**Further Reading:**

- *Alcorn, Randy. Managing God's Money: A Biblical Guide. Carol Stream, IL: Tyndale, 2011.*

- *_____. Money, Possessions, and Eternity: A Comprehensive Guide to What the Bible Says about Financial Stewardship, Generosity, Materialism, Retirement, Financial Planning, Gambling, Debt, and More. Carol Stream, IL: Tyndale, 2021.*

- *DeMoss, Nancy. Choosing Gratitude: Your Journey to Joy. Chicago, IL: Moody, 2009.*

- *Evans, Tony. Kingdom Stewardship. Carol Stream, IL: Tyndale, 2020.*

- *Tripp, Paul David. Redeeming Money: How God Reveals and Reorients Our Hearts. Wheaton, IL: Crossway, 2018.*

- *_____. Sex and Money: Pleasures That Leave You Empty and Grace that Satisfies. Wheaton, IL: Crossway, 2013.*

# The Idol of Self-Care

"DEMAND WHAT YOU DESERVE."
"EMBRACE YOUR FLAWS."
"EXERCISE MORE."
"FOLLOW YOUR OWN PATH."
"SET BOUNDARIES."
"CLEAN YOURSELF UP."
"TREAT YOURSELF."

Self-care culture is not godly wisdom. At best, it is a marketing technique that taps into your selfishness. At worst, it is a new set of laws to enslave your soul.

These mantras present a whole bunch of ways for you to feel like a failure. Do you see the number of times "you" is front and center? While this may seem like a no-nonsense approach to life, you cannot empower yourself to be happy. It took all of one second for marketers to realize that #selfcare sells stuff. From candles to at-home spa junk, every brand has realized the power of slapping #selfcare or #treatyoself onto their items.

These mantras ring hollow because they have no meaning. One popular blogger tells you, "Eating indulgently can help your mental state," while another says, "Eating well balances you out." Which is it? Everything is self-care now -- staying in or going out with friends, working out or resting, lots of makeup, or throwing your makeup away. Opportunity after opportunity to fail. When you indulge, you feel fat. When you work out, you wonder why the results aren't coming fast enough and feel like you are depriving yourself. These sayings represent a never-ending cycle of failure. They are a burden no one should be carrying.

If modern self-care had a tagline, I think it would be this: *I'll be happy once the universe is ordered around me.* There are two problems with that statement. One, you will never be able to truly order your life around yourself unless you are okay being by yourself. Two, and most importantly, you cannot make yourself happy. There is not a hidden corner of your soul containing joy that is waiting to be found. You can distract yourself, yes. The majority of self-care items for sale are distractions. The majority of self-care advice is meant to distract. My heart breaks for the millions of broken people distracting themselves to death. There are over 59 million posts on Instagram using #selfcare. Do you think they will eventually distract themselves into joy? Let's heed Paul's warning, "She who is self-indulgent is dead even while she lives."[28]

Eternal joy is available to you -- but it isn't inside of you waiting to be discovered.

I think we often forget who we are. If you are a Christian, it is tragic when you forget *whose* you are. **Christian, you belong to**

---

[28]1 Timothy 5:6 (ESV).

**Jesus.** He purchased you with His precious blood. When you put your trust in Him, you received His righteousness. This is what the Father sees when He looks at you -- a beloved son or daughter. This is reality. Our emotions in our fallen bodies are at war, often with the truth. The Spirit of God must change our feelings to align with this glorious reality.

Hear me clearly: You need to take care of yourself. I am not encouraging you to fill your life with people who run you over, saying you never need time alone, or you should be content with being unproductive and lazy. "Self-care," as our culture understands it, is not a call to take care of the bodies and lives the Lord has given us. We should all do that and ask the Spirit to encourage us in it. Exercise CAN help with the physical effects of anxiety and depression. Eating well DOES positively affect your brain chemistry. Good sleep habits DO help you think clearer in your battle against anxiety and depression. My point here is this: spend more time meditating on the paragraph above and sitting in the reality of who you are in Christ, rather than trying to find happiness and joy in a good day off. The kind of love that changes the world is not "self-love," but "self-sacrificing love."

**Further Reading in Scripture:**
- Psalm 4:8
- Matthew 11:28-30
- Hebrews 4:9-11

**Reflection:**

1. What activities/moments do you consider to be "self-care" for you?
2. Are the above activities/moments God-centered or radically self-centered?
3. Consider the last paragraph of this devotional. How can you balance taking care of yourself well and serving/loving others in a healthy way?

**Further Reading:**

- Comer, John Mark. *The Ruthless Elimination of Hurry: How to Stay Emotionally Healthy and Spiritually Alive in the Chaos of the Modern World.* Colorado Springs, CO: WaterBrook, 2019.
- Scazzero, Peter. *Emotionally Healthy Spirituality: It's Impossible to Be Spiritually Mature, While Remaining Emotionally Immature.* Grand Rapids, MI: Zondervan, 2017.
- Wirzba, Norman. *Living the Sabbath: Discovering the Rhythms of Rest and Delighti.* Grand Rapids, MI: Brazos Press, 2006.

## The Idol of Appearance & Health

Research finds that, when asked, 80 percent or more of people say they are not content with their appearance.[29] We've already dealt with the idol of social media, but even those who are not influenced by it can still be tempted to make an idol out of their appearance or overall health. Before we begin, the Bible is clear on the fact that we should take care of our bodies.

> *Don't you know that your body is a temple of the*
> *Holy Spirit who is in you, whom you have from*
> *God? You are not your own, for you were bought*
> *at a price. So glorify God with your body.*[30]

Sloth is a sin -- careless overeating and binging is idolatry of food and drink -- and the Scriptures are clear. We should take care of the bodies God has given us; it is just good stewardship. But that care can easily become an obsession, an idol. Just look at the sheer amount of money spent in the fitness industry in the western world. In 2020, the market size of the gym, health, and fitness club industry in the United States was estimated at over 32 billion U.S. dollars.[31] Think about the advertisements you see on social media and TV -- vitamins, energy drinks, at-home gym equipment, diet plans, prepared meals, etc. We've all known individuals who bow

---

[29](Psychology Today).
[30]1 Corinthians 6:19-20 (CSB).
[31](Statista, 2021).

before this idol. If you ever find yourself experiencing constant tiredness, "living" at the gym, and feeling anxiety and guilt over missing a workout, you might be worshiping a false god.

Let the Apostle Paul (who is writing in this passage to a young pastor, Timothy) straighten out our thinking.

> *But have nothing to do with pointless and silly myths. Rather, train yourself in godliness. For the training of the body has limited benefit, but godliness is beneficial in every way, since it holds promise for the present life and also for the life to come.*[32]

Staying in good physical shape has limited benefit. Spiritual health is eternal. Many worship this idol in an attempt to get attention from those they are attracted to, and to feel worthy. This was shared in another topic, but it bears repeating -- your greatest need is not a romantic relationship or attention from an individual. Your greatest need is to know and follow Jesus. Only He can bring about abiding peace and joy in your life.

"When the heart desires lustful attention, no amount of external rules will affect the heart. When the heart desires God, the heart will be modest and external rules will not be needed."[33]

---

[32] 1 Timothy 4:7-8 (CSB).
[33] *Modesty: More Than a Change of Clothes*, 110.

Your worth in the eyes of God is not contingent on your physical appearance or overall health. It is a lie from hell that has convinced millions (maybe billions) that western advertisers can tell us who is beautiful and who is not. How can you be set free from this guilt and shame? Run to the only one who has *made* you beautiful by His blood shed for you: Jesus. Listen to the true standard of beauty:

> *Don't let your beauty consist of outward things like elaborate hairstyles and wearing gold jewelry or fine clothes, **but rather what is inside the heart** -- the imperishable quality of a gentle and quiet spirit, which is of great worth in God's sight.*[34]

**Further Reading in Scripture:**
- Psalm 139:14
- Matthew 23:28
- Ephesians 2:10
- 1 Timothy 2:9-10

**Reflection:**
1. Do you spend so much time prepping your appearance that you forget to prepare your heart each day?
2. Do you realize that, ultimately, all appearances and physical forms of beauty are temporary?

---

[34] 1 Peter 3:3-4 (CSB).

3. Discuss how you view yourself in the mirror - in all your physical "inadequacies" -- Christian -- does God not just see His son or daughter? Why enslave yourself to the fallible opinions of humans?

**Further Readings:**

- Peace, Martha, and Keller, Kent. *Modesty: More Than a Change of Clothes.* Phillipsburg, NJ: P&R Publishing Co., 2015.

- Smith, Jesse. *Restoring Christian Modesty: God's Perfect Will for Your Outward Appearance.* Mitchellville, MD: Bride of Christ Ministries, 2019.

- Vaughn, David J., and Diane Vaughan. *The Beauty of Modesty: Cultivating Virtue in the Face of a Vulgar Culture.* Nashville, TN: Cumberland House, 2005.

## The Idol of Your Heart

If you want to understand what a culture values and believes, watch their advertisements. *Coca-Cola* perfectly captured our self-centered western culture in their 2018 Super-Bowl advertisement. Here's an excerpt if you didn't see it:

*"Look, here's the thing about Diet Coke. It's delicious. It makes me feel good. Life is short. If you want to live in a yurt, yurt it up. If you want to run in a marathon, I mean, that sounds super hard, but OK. I mean, just do you...."*

They tweeted, "Because 'you do you' is our mantra. #becauseIcan."

Disney "self-esteem" initiatives and the media have been encouraging people to follow their hearts for a few generations now. The results have been disastrous. **Our hearts, apart from new life in Christ, lead us joyfully into sin.** *It is death to self, not embracing yourself, that leads to life!*[35]

> "The heart is deceitful above all things, and desperately sick; who can understand it?"[36]

---

[35]Matthew 16:25, Luke 9:23 (ESV).
[36]Jeremiah 17:9 (ESV).

Your heart cannot be trusted. Your heart is not missing something. Your heart, apart from Jesus, is dead. Instead of encouraging people to follow their dead, rebellious hearts, we should be saying, *you need a new heart!* Only Jesus can take our hearts of stone and replace them with hearts of flesh (Ezek. 36:26). We need new hearts that have a desire for holiness and a love for Jesus and people. Then, and only then, can we be freed from the penalty of our sinful nature. If you are born again, know that you are still at war with your sin. **Your heart can still deceive you.** But now, with the Spirit of God in you, you can say "n"o to sin. Don't blindly follow your desires. Kill the sin that still dwells within you.

**Further Reading in Scripture:**
- Psalm 14:1
- Matthew 5:28
- Matthew 15:19

**Reflection:**
1. What is the most dangerous thing/feeling/belief to which your heart led you?
2. Read Psalm 139 and see David asking God to *search his heart*. David is saying, "show me where you want me to grow in holiness, God." Discuss what that means for your life. Are you willing to genuinely ask God to reveal sin in your life?
3. Discuss what it means for you to have a *new heart* (Ezek. 36). If you are a Christian, what desires have changed since God saved you? From what sin do you experience less

temptation? Christian, you should celebrate this work of God in your life! Remind yourself how far Jesus has brought you. Let this reminder encourage you to continue to confess and repent of sin. "If we confess our sins, he is faithful and righteous to forgive us our sins and to cleanse us from all unrighteousness."[37]

## Further Readings:

- Bridges, Jerry. *The Pursuit of Holiness*. Colorado Springs, CO: NavPress, 2006.
- Comer, John Mark. *Live No Lies: Recognize and Resist the Three Enemies that Sabotage Your Peace*. Colorado Springs, CO: WaterBrook, 2021.
- Lawson, Steven J. *It Will Cost Your Everything: What it Takes to Follow Jesus*. Fearn: Christian Focus Publications, 2021.
- Platt, David. *Follow Me: A Call to Die. A Call to Live*. Carol Stream, IL: Tyndale House, 2013.
- Tozer, A. W. *The Pursuit of God*. Harrisburg, PA: Christian Publications, Inc., 2015.

---

[37] 1 John 1:9 (CSB).

# The Idol of Sex & Pornography

I once heard a story about the British journalist Malcolm Muggeridge. One morning, he saw a woman bathing across the river during his usual swim. Living away from his wife, he saw an opportunity he could not pass up. Thinking that no one would ever know, he swam upstream toward the woman. His mind fed him the fantasy that stolen waters would be sweet, and he swam harder for it. Swimming underwater, Muggeridge surfaced near the woman, and what he saw gave him the shock of a lifetime: The woman was a leper. "Her nose was eaten away. There were sores and white blotches all over her skin, and the ends of her fingers were gone. She looked more like an animal than a human. She grinned at me, showing a toothless mask. "'What a wretched woman this is,' [Muggeridge] thought to himself, but at the same moment, he was overwhelmed with a devastating truth: 'What a wretched man I am!'"[38]

The grass is never greener on the other side. Everyone -- teenagers, single young people, married folks -- we are all tempted to dream about the "what ifs." These wandering wicked thoughts come from our hearts. Jesus said in Matthew 15:19 and 20: "Out of the heart come evil thoughts, murders, adulteries, fornications, thefts, false witness, slanders. These are the things which defile the man."[39] And then He said, "The evil man out of the evil treasure of his

---

[38]Dr. Young, Ed.
[39]Matthew 15:19-20 (ESV).

heart brings forth what is evil, for his mouth speaks from that which fills his heart."[40] This is why yesterday's devotional is so important. You cannot wish away your sinful feelings. **You and I need divine intervention to fight sin.**

"God has given us this whole dimension in life -- making us sexual beings and giving us this instinct towards lifelong partnership -- precisely to point us to the deeper and greater reality of his covenant love for us in Christ. This dimension to live, like all others, is distorted and diminished by our having turned from God. Our sexual feelings are disordered and often inappropriate; we don't keep our promises; and we make sex about fulfilling our own appetites. But the basic shape remains. Our sexuality is meant to point us to the deeper yearning, the fuller satisfaction, and the greater consummation that comes from knowing Jesus"[41]

Sex is a gift from God. Sex makes a terrible and soul-destroying god. **To pursue sex outside of monogamous, heterosexual marriage will bring ruin to your life.** To pursue sex on a screen will bring ruin to your life. Studies on the effects of pornography are in infancy. We may never truly know the damage widespread porn exposure has had on gen x and millennials. The average age of exposure is now 9 in the United States. Porn destroys marriages. It warps, deceives, and enslaves men and women. If you struggle with this, think about the damage it has done to your life. **If you**

---

[40]Luke 6:45 (NIV).
[41]Allberry, Sam, *Why Does God Care Who I Sleep With?*, 134-135.

**have not been found out yet, know that you will. Sin always rises to the surface.**

If you are struggling, let me encourage you with a few things Christian counselors have found that work: 1. Get rid of your smartphone, OR have your parents/accountability partner password lock all apps. Get a dumbphone. Jesus said, if your right hand causes you to sin, cut it off. **Quit playing with your sin by having a smartphone around;** 2. Eliminate all other points of access (e.g., smart TV, game consoles, etc.) and live out in the open with your struggles with your family and Christian community. You should not fight sin alone.

*The "stop looking at porn" gospel is weak. You need the real thing. The true gospel rewires you. It convicts you instantaneously. It breeds repentance. It helps you hate sin, crucify the flesh, and build discipline. It targets weakness in character.*

*We need a "know Jesus savingly so that your sin is washed away and you have a new nature and now hate sin and wake up every morning eager to hunt it down where it sleeps" gospel.*[42]

---

[42] Strachan, Owen.

**Further Reading in Scripture:**

- Romans 6:11-14
- 1 Corinthians 6:18
- 1 Corinthians 10:13
- Ephesians 5:3
- 1 Thessalonians 4:3-5

**Reflection**:

1.  Be honest -- do you struggle with sexual sin?
2.  Who needs to know about your struggles with this sin today? You should not fight sin alone.
3.  Have you tried to destroy this idol with your own power -- or have you relied on the Holy Spirit to change your heart and desires?

**Further Readings:**

- Allender, Dan B. *Healing the Wounded Heart: The Heartache of Sexual Abuse and the Hope of Transformation*. Grand Rapids, MI: Baker Books, 2016.
- Kell, J. Garrett. *Pure in Heart: Sexual Sin and the Promises of God*. Wheaton, IL: Crossway, 2021.
- Ortlund, Raymond. *The Death of Porn: Men of Integrity Building a World of Nobility*. Wheaton, IL: Crossway, 2021.
- Rigney, Joe. *More Than a Battle: How to Experience Victory, Freedom, and Healing from Lust*. Nashville, TN: B&H Publishing, 2021.
- Stringer, Jay. *Unwanted: How Sexual Brokenness Reveals Our Way to Healing*. Colorado Springs, CO: NavPress, 2018.
- Tripp, Paul David *Sex and Money: Pleasures That Leave You Empty and Grace that Satisfies*. Wheaton, IL: Crossway, 2013.

# The Idol of Relationships

*If I could just find my soulmate, I'd be happy.*

Let's consider that statement. Do you truly believe that finding another sinner to share your life with will fix your problems? Consider all your sinful habits and patterns. Every other individual has those as well. The joining of two lives is a messy matter. Marriage is a gift from the Lord, and it is a lifelong project. Marriage is not eternal bliss and happiness. Jesus is. **Your greatest need is not a boyfriend/girlfriend/spouse. It is Jesus.**

I don't mean this in some kind of strange *Jesus is your physical spouse* nonsense. What I mean is, only Jesus can make you eternally happy. Another sinner will never be able to say, "I see you completely. I forgive you completely. Because of my sacrifice, the Father accepts you completely." Only Jesus can. Can you see how that kind of "knowing" is a clear parallel to what marriage is supposed to be though?

Marriage exists to display the mystery and beauty of the relationship between Christ and His bride, the church.

In a healthy marriage between two Christians, the world sees a picture of Jesus' love for His bride. That's the design for marriage.

In a devotional about relationships, why am I talking about marriage so much? Because there is no biblical category for boyfriends and girlfriends. Scripture teaches that you are under the authority of your parents, and then at marriage, *two become one flesh* (Gen 2:24). Does this mean dating is unbiblical? No. Not if by "dating" you mean the process of getting to know someone and their family/friends in hopes of marriage. As you read in the *idol of sex* devotional earlier, the modern hyper-sexualized dating scene is soul-destroying. I don't say that because I am old-fashioned. I say that because everyone who walks out of that lifestyle attests to it. You were not made to be a product or an experience that is consumed by countless strangers. You were made to be known and loved in a covenant relationship.

**Now, some advice:**
Young women, hear me clearly:

If your boyfriend hates authority, is constantly in conflict with his teachers or boss, thinks everyone else is an idiot but him, hates all forms of authority, defies his parents openly, refuses to join a church -- do NOT marry him.

Anyone who refuses to be under authority (church/boss/school) will be a terrible spouse.

Young men, hear me clearly:

You are not worthy of being a husband if you are like the boy mentioned above or are addicted to pornography. Seek older, godly men to walk with you and kill sin by the Spirit's power.

**Further Reading in Scripture**:

- Genesis 2:24
- 1 Corinthians 7:1-40
- 2 Corinthians 6:14
- Ephesians 5:22-33
- Hebrews 13:4

**Questions**:

1. When have you tried to find happiness in another person?
2. How did that go for you?

*A note for those who struggle with sexual sin or have been abused*:

Your sexual sin does not define you. Any sin that's been done against you sexually does not define you. If you belong to Jesus, what He has done defines you. Don't believe the lies of the Enemy that say you are dirty, unworthy of love, and broken beyond repair. You are clean, washed, and made new in Him. He has taken your filthy rags and given you His righteous robes![43]

---

[43]Pastor Keeney, Ryan, https://gracechurchsw.com/

**Further Readings:**

- Bethke, Jefferson, and Alyssa Bethke. *Love That Lasts: How We Discovered God's Better Way for Love, Dating, Marriage, and Sex.* Nashville, TN: HarperCollins Publishers, 2017.
- Comer, John Mark. *Loveology: God. Love. Marriage. Sex. And the Never-Ending Story of Male and Female.* Grand Rapids, MI: Zondervan, 2014.
- Keller, Timothy, and Kathy Keller *The Meaning of Marriage: Facing the Complexities of Commitment with the Wisdom of God.* New York, NY: Penguin Books, 2013.
- Stanley, Andy. *The New Rules for Love, Sex, and Dating.* Grand Rapids, MI: Zondervan, 2014.
- Stuart, Ben. *Single, Dating, Engaged, Married: Navigating Life and Love in the Modern Age.* Nashville, TN: HarperCollins Publishers, 2017.
- Tripp, Paul David. *What Did You Expect?: Redeeming the Realities of Marriage.* Wheaton, IL: Crossway, 2010.

# The Idol of Comfort

Is your mood dependent on the amount of free time you have week to week? Do you dislike people who intrude on your phone scrolling? Do you lash out at people when they interrupt your entertainment?

> "Sodom's sins were pride, gluttony, and laziness, while the poor and needy suffered outside her door."[44]

You could replace Sodom with any modern nation. We love our air-conditioned fortresses. Many of us do not even know our neighbor's or classmates' names. Most big churches have become a drive-thru hour of encouragement: no gospel, no calls to die to self, and only comfortable preaching. We go home, get on our phones, and repeat next Sunday. This is the wicked opposite of what we see in the book of Acts. The early disciples shared their possessions (Acts 4:32-35), met each other's needs, and met *more than once a week (Acts 2:46)*. How can you obey the command to "bear each other's burdens" if you are primarily concerned with your own comfort? Do you know the pains, joys, and hopes of those with whome you go to church/youth group? If not, compare your life with the book of Acts. Compare your *church or youth group* to the fellowship of believers in the book of Acts.

---

[44]Ezekiel 16:49 (NLT).

When was the last time you proclaimed the Gospel to someone? Does the fear of being uncomfortable or seen as strange keep you from telling others about Jesus? Our comfort should be of no concern when souls are on the steps of hell.

**Jesus promises us rest. But this is not the same thing as glutinous comfort.** Jesus left the ultimate comfort, the throne of heaven, to come to us. To prioritize our comfort is to prioritize ourselves. Loving comfort is selfish pride.

Our culture teaches us to avoid pain and discomfort. But God often uses pain and discomfort to grow and shape us to be more like Jesus. The Bible does not teach us to jump headlong into pain like a masochist, but instead to embrace the trials God sends our way for our good (James 1:2-4). If you are a genuine Christian, you will experience persecution and suffering (2 Tim. 3:12, Luke 14:27, Rom. 8:18). Don't be so quick to run to comfortable things/people and miss out on what God might be doing in your discomfort.

> "God is far more concerned with your Christlikeness than your comfort."[45]

Can you and I say with Job,

*It would still bring me comfort,*
*and I would leap for joy in unrelenting pain*

---

[45]Begg, Alistair.

*that I have not denied the words of the Holy One.*[46]

**Further Reading in Scripture:**
- Psalm 119:50
- Isaiah 51:12
- Matthew 11:28-30
- Revelation 21:4

**Reflection:**

1. Read 2 Timothy 3:12, Luke 14:27, and Romans 8:18. Discuss what it looks like for you to suffer for Jesus. Do you find yourself in awkward conversations about faith? Turning down invitations to parties where you will be tempted to sin? Left out of group texts because you follow Jesus? Ostracized by old friends because of your Christian morals?

2. What or whom do you run to when you need "comforting"? Examples: social media, boyfriend/girlfriend, video games, food, pornography, social events, etc.

3. What would it look like for God to become your source of great comfort? How do prayer and Scripture memory factor into that? Read Matthew 11:28-30. Do you believe that?

---

[46]Job 6:10 (CSB).

**Further Readings:**

- Hildreth, Scott, and Steven A. McKinion. *Sharing Jesus without Freaking Out: Evangelism the Way You Were Born to Do It*. Nashville, TN: B&H Academic, 2020.
- Luck, Kenny. *Risk: Are You Willing to Trust God with Everything?*. Colorado Springs, CO: WaterBrook, 2006.
- Platt, David. *Radical: Taking Back Your Faith from the American Dream*. Colorado Springs, CO: Multnomah Books, 2010.
- Piper, John. *Don't Waste Your Life*. Wheaton, IL: Crossway, 2009.
- Willis, Dustin, and Aaron Coe. *Life on Mission: Joining the Everyday Mission of God*. Chicago, IL: Moody Publishers, 2014.

# The Idol of Security & Safety

My local sports radio station is sponsored by a home security company. Day in and day out, I've heard their ads and taglines, "What's more important than keeping your family safe?" "Don't compromise on your kid's safety." "Show your family you love them with the gift of security." As a father of three young children, my wife and I feel this pressure. The Bible clearly commands us to take care of our families (1 Tim. 5:8), but Jesus also says, "It is better to lose your life than to keep it (John 12:25)." The advancement of God's kingdom is worthy of *our* lives because King Jesus gave up *His*.

Real Christianity is not "safe". C. S. Lewis captured this perfectly in his book, "The Lion, the Witch and the Wardrobe," when Lucy asks Mrs. Beaver about Aslan (the Christ-figure in those novels), "Is this lion safe? Oh no, said Mrs. Beaver, He is not safe, but He is good! He's the King I tell you!"

Jesus never promised us worldly safety. In fact, He prepared us for the opposite. He said: "In this world you will have trouble"; "Do not be surprised if they hate you, they hated me first"; "You will be thrown in front of the officials"; etc., etc. The message is clear: authentic Christianity could get us killed.

Authentic Christianity can also get us ridiculed, shamed, and *canceled*. There is quickly coming a day where basic Christian ethics will be abhorrent to the culture around us. Christian sexual ethics are already seen as hate-filled bigotry.

There's not enough room in this devotional to share what Christians throughout history have lost to maintain their witness. Are you prepared to lose your job, friends, respect from the world, maybe even your life for Jesus?

Jesus said in John 15:18-20:

> *If the world hates you, understand that it hated me before it hated you. If you were of the world, the world would love you as its own. However, because you are not of the world, but I have chosen you out of it, the world hates you. Remember the word I spoke to you: 'A servant is not greater than his master.' If they persecuted me, they will also persecute you. If they kept my word, they will also keep yours.*[47]

What *did* Jesus promise us regarding eternal safety? He said; "No one will be able to snatch you out of my hands,"[48] and "take heart, I have overcome the world."[49]

---

[47]John 15:18-20 (CSB).
[48]John 10:28 (CSB).
[49]John 16:33 (CSB).

My kids, and your future kids, do not belong to us. They belong to God. I struggle with this. I feel like a failure if one of my kids gets hurt when I'm near them. But Jesus could call them to die in a foreign nation (or their own) for His name.

Jesus has called *us all* to die (Luke 9:23). He calls us to die to self, sinful desires, and worldly motivations. I believe we all have a deep desire for adventure and joining up with a movement bigger than ourselves. The gospel fulfills these needs. We were made for this adventure of God's redemptive plan! Jesus is worthy of your life.

**Further Reading in Scripture:**
- Matthew 10:16
- Romans 8:35
- James 4:4

**Reflection:**
1. Have you ever done something wrong because of peer pressure? It always feels "safer" to go with the crowd instead of standing out.
2. Do you know any stories of those who have lost their lives because they wouldn't reject Jesus or deny a basic truth of Christianity? Read *Jesus Freaks - The Voice of the Martyrs* for some amazing stories from the faithful.
3. Are you sure of your salvation in Jesus? If someone took your life, would you be with Him?

**Further Readings:**

- Hildreth, Scott, and Steven A. McKinion. *Sharing Jesus Without Freaking Out: Evangelism the Way You Were Born to Do It.* Nashville, TN: B&H Academic, 2020.
- Luck, Kenny. *Risk: Are You Willing to Trust God with Everything?.* Colorado Springs, CO: WaterBrook, 2006.
- Platt, David. *Radical: Taking Back Your Faith from the American Dream.* Colorado Springs, CO: Multnomah Books, 2010.
- Piper, John. *Don't Waste Your Life.* Wheaton, IL: Crossway, 2009.
- Willis, Dustin, and Aaron Coe. *Life on Mission: Joining the Everyday Mission of God.* Chicago, IL: Moody Publishers, 2014.

# The Idol of Power & Social Media

Social media has ruined many lives. Its negative effects on us are just now being compiled and studied by psychologists. Everyone knows someone who has had their sleep, body image, or "real life" social interactions wrecked by social media. That person might even be you.

Social media is our feeble attempt to convince the world we have it all together. After all, everyone wants to be famous. We create a "highlight reel" for everyone to see, *or* we carefully cultivate a victim persona so everyone can feel sorry for us. The pendulum can swing to either extreme. The unifying sin, in either case, is this: when *other people's* view of us becomes *our identity.*

Finding value and worth in other people's opinions will never make you happy. *Your worth is not rooted in your appearance, your accomplishments, or your family tree.* Your worth is rooted in the fact that you were created in the image of God. You will never get enough "likes" to feel validated by other sinners.

Gaining popularity and power won't fix you. We have thousands of years of human history to prove that. Governments and individuals seeking power have cost hundreds of millions of people their lives. All the images and statues and billboards crumble in the end.

*It matters not how strait the gate,*

   *How charged with punishments the scroll,*

*I am the master of my fate,*

   *I am the captain of my soul.*[50]

This is an easy illusion to believe. The bravado is a rush to our sad souls. Consider Jesus:

*Though he was in the form of God, did not count equality with God a thing to be grasped, but emptied himself, by taking the form of a servant, being born in the likeness of men.*[51]

John Piper says, "Christ moved from heavenly heights to such shameful degradation on our behalf." Should Christians be a people seeking after power, as individuals or corporately? No. We deny ourselves, not caring what the world thinks of us. By the power of the Spirit, we keep our consciences clean and live at peace with everyone (Rom. 12:18). Do not create a kingdom for yourself, it will fade away (Dan. 2:44).

   "If you follow Christ, the world will unfollow you."[52]

---

[50]Henley, William Ernest.
[51]Philippians 2:6--7 (ESV).
[52]Reinke, Tony, *12 Ways Your Phone Is Changing You.*

**Further Reading in Scripture:**
- Psalm 119:10
- Jeremiah 29:13
- Zephaniah 2:3
- Matthew 6:33
- Luke 11:9-10

**Reflection:**
1. What have you done on social media to become the person you want the world to see?
2. Does the above "persona" honor God?

**Further Readings:**
- Detweiler, Craig. *iGods: How Technology Shapes Our Spiritual and Social Lives.* Grand Rapids, MI: Brazos Press, 2013.
- Kizer, Drew. *Dangerous Playground: The Christian and Social Media.* Leeds, AL: Riddle Creek Publishing, 2019.
- McCracken, Brett. *The Wisdom Pyramid: Feeding Your Soul in a Post-Truth World.* Wheaton, IL: Crossway, 2021.
- Reinke, Tony. *12 Ways Your Phone is Changing You.* Wheaton, IL: Crossway, 2017.
- _____. *Competing Spectacles: Treasuring Christ in the Media Age.* Wheaton, IL: Crossway, 2019.
- Turkle, Sherry. *Alone Together: Why We Expect More from Technology and Less from Each Other.* Philadelphia, PA: Basic Books, 2011.

# The Idol of Acceptance (The Fear of Man)

This devotional is almost a "part two" of yesterday's thoughts. Instead of considering what social media does to our souls, today we will look at the deeper idol of acceptance that drives much of what we do online.

Many of us have been crippled by the question, *"What do they think of me?"*

"The fear of man lays a snare, but whoever trusts in the Lord is safe."[53] The Hebrew word here for "snare" refers to traps hunters used to catch animals or birds.

We were created to seek approval. It is natural for us to want someone to say, *"Well done."* But seeking the approval of people can lead to sin. When you seek the approval of others, it can lead to misunderstandings and hurt feelings. Only Jesus can give us the approval we desire and need.

> *For am I now seeking the approval of man, or of God? Or am I trying to please man? If I were still trying to please man, I would not be a servant of Christ.*[54]

---

[53]Proverbs 29:25 (ESV).
[54] Galatians 1:10 (ESV).

There are two directions we can go with this idolatry. Some of us care so much about what people think that we will do whatever we can to be liked. Others fear people so much that they won't do anything and be passive in life.

Both options keep us from living an abundant life in God's presence.

You were created to live in the approving light of your heavenly Father. This is possible because of Jesus' life, death, and resurrection! Do you know that you can please your Father in heaven?

> *Dear friends, if our hearts don't condemn us, we have confidence before God and receive whatever we ask from him because we keep his commands and do what is pleasing in his sight.*[55]

We can follow his commandments because His Spirit is in us! I can only imagine the joy of the Father watching His newly adopted children submitting to His rule and reign. Knowing that my Father delights in my obedience quells any fear of what people might think. Rest in His gladness over you, Christian.

*The Lord your God is among you,*
*a warrior who saves.*

---

[55]1 John 3:21-22 (CSB).

*He will rejoice over you with gladness.*
*He will be quiet in his love.*
*He will delight in you with singing.*[56]

If you are not a born-again disciple of Jesus, the above verse is not true for you. At this point in this devotional, I want to ask again: Have you trusted in Christ alone to save you and deliver you from your wicked heart that produces these idols?

**Further Reading in Scripture:**
- John 3:16
- Romans 8:31-39
- Romans 11:15
- 1 Timothy 1:15
- 1 John 1:9

**Reflection:**
1. Right now, who do you want to be seen/accepted/loved by?
2. Consider what the Father sees when He looks at you (Christian). He sees the perfect obedience and righteousness of Jesus, the Beloved Son!
3. Have you ever found lasting satisfaction in the approval of other humans, or have they inevitably disappointed you?

---

[56]Zephaniah 3:17 (CSB).

**Further Readings:**

- Bridges, Jerry. *Who Am I?: Identity in Christ*. Adelphi, MD: Cruciform Press, 2012.

- Kruger, Melissa. *Identity Theft: Reclaiming the Truth of Who We Are in Christ*. Deerfield, IL: The Gospel Coalition, 2018.

- Rosner, Brian S. *Known by God: A Biblical Theology of Personal Identity*. Grand Rapids, MI: Zondervan, 2017.

- Welch, Edward. *When People Are Big and God is Small: Overcoming Peer Pressure, Codependency, and the Fear of Man*. Phillipsburg, NJ: P&R Publishing Co., 1997.

## The Idol of Naturalism

Modern people believe that they are the lords of this world. A common intellectual barrier to the Gospel is the belief that science has the power to explain everything in the universe. Who needs God? Maybe you even find the world less *magical* the older you get. That is not the result of your increasing knowledge. That is the result of your increasing naturalism. Naturalism is a worldview that teaches only natural laws and natural forces operate in the world. The more a Christian believes in naturalism, the less dependent they become on God.

Naturalism feeds pride but creates a dead world. No one lives like they are a carbon sack on a spinning rock. Things matter. Love is real. Stories and songs move us. We care for each other and get angry when we see injustice.

Don't let this dangerous worldview creep into your heart. Remember God's design of the universe. Remember the reality of the supernatural realm. Jesus performed miracles, drove out demons, and rose from the dead physically.

Naturalism has no place in Christianity. The created world is indeed amazing, but the *heavens declare the glory of God.*[57]

---

[57]Psalm 19:1 (ESV).

Look at the top movies over the last 20 years. Nearly all of them involve the supernatural and otherworldly. Why is that? Because the average person is starved for something beyond themselves. C. S. Lewis (the author of the *Narnia* series among others) recognized this in his work, *The Screwtape Letters,* almost eighty years ago. In this fictional letter, a senior demon is writing to his nephew about how to tempt and lead humans astray.

> *My Dear Wormwood,*
>
> *Our policy, for the moment, is to conceal ourselves. Of course this has not always been so. We are really faced with a cruel dilemma. When the humans disbelieve in our existence we lose all the pleasing results of direct terrorism and we make no magicians. On the other hand, when they believe in us, we cannot make them materialists and sceptics.*[58]

The world trains us to be materialists and skeptics. You might even function that way. Pray and ask that God will make known His hand in creation and our individual lives. We need a clear view of Scripture to help us not discount or reinterpret its numerous miraculous passages. Ask the Spirit to make His gracious, manifest presence known. Remember that you, Christian, are at war....

---

[58]Lewis, C. S., *The Screwtape Letters.*

*For we do not wrestle against flesh and blood,*
*but against the rulers, against the authorities,*
*against the cosmic powers over this present*
*darkness, against the spiritual forces of evil in*
*the heavenly places.*[59]

**Further Reading in Scripture:**
- Job 12:7-10
- Job 37:14-16
- Psalm 19:1
- Psalm 104:24-25
- Romans 1:20

**Reflection:**
1. Do you doubt some of the Bible's supernatural accounts (think: the virgin birth of Christ, crossing the Red Sea, the dead raised, demonic activity, fire from heaven, walking on water, etc.)?
2. What do you do with those doubts?
3. Is belief in the supernatural a barrier to Christianity for you (non-believers)?

**Further Readings:**
- Chester, Tim. *Do Miracles Happen Today?*. Charlotte, NC: The Good Book Company, 2020.

---

[59]Ephesians 6:12 (ESV).

- Deere, Jack S. *Why I Am Still Surprised by the Power of the Spirit: Discovering How God Speaks and Heals Today.* Grand Rapids, MI: Zondervan, 2020.
- Dembski, William, and Sean McDowell. *Understanding Intelligent Design: Everything You Need to Know in Plain Language.* Eugene OR: Harvest House, 2008.
- Lennox, John. *Can Science Explain Everything?.* Charlotte, NC: The Good Book Company, 2019.
- _____. *God's Undertaker: Has Science Buried God?.* Oxford: Lion Books, 2009
- Moreland, J. P. *Christianity and the Nature of Science.* Grand Rapids, MI: Baker Books, 1989.
- _____. *Scientism and Secularism: Learning to Respond to a Dangerous Ideology.* Wheaton, IL: Crossway, 2018.
- Ortlund, Gavin. *Why God Makes Sense in a World That Doesn't: The Beauty of Christian Theism.* Grand Rapids, MI: Baker Academic, 2021.
- Strobel, Lee. *The Case for Miracles: A Journalist Investigates Evidence for the Supernatural.* Grand Rapids, MI: Zondervan, 2018.

## The Idol of Stuff (Consumerism)

There are 300,000 items in the average American home.[60]

The average American generates 52 tons of garbage by age 75.[61]

The average American throws away 65 pounds of clothing per year.[62]

The United States has upward of 50,000 storage facilities, over five times the number of Starbucks. Currently, there are 7.3 square feet of self-storage space for every man, woman, and child in the nation. Thus, it is physically possible that every American could stand--all at the same time--under the total canopy of self-storage roofing (SSA).

We are drowning in stuff. America's children are taught from the earliest age to be rabid consumers. America's adults are trained to buy the newest model of something every year. I am thankful to God to have access to the most productive technology in human history. I also acknowledge how easily I slip into worshiping things. Have you ever obsessed over the newest ____? Fully convinced yourself that you didn't just *want* it, you *needed* it?

---

[60]Los Angeles Times.
[61]Washington State University.
[62]Huffington Post.

Maybe you said to yourself, *I deserve this.* Jesus said, "where your treasure is, there your heart will be also."[63]

**The hammer that destroys the idol of consumerism is *gratefulness.*** You are blessed. As you read this, consider what the Lord has given you today. We get so hung up on our wants that we often forget how Jesus provides *everything we need.* If you are filled with gratitude, you have no room for wanting what is not yours.

Jon Bloom says it this way,

> *The more thankfulness is present in us, the less vulnerable we are to sin. That's why the Bible talks so much about thanksgiving. Thankful people have set their eyes on God (Heb. 12:2), recognizing to some degree how much grace we are receiving right now (2 Cor. 9:8), trusting him to cover all our sin and work our painful past for good (Rom. 8:28), and looking to him for all we need tomorrow and into eternity (Phil. 4:19). Souls that learn to be content in God "in whatever situation" (Phil 4:11) are souls that are the least vulnerable to temptation, particularly covetous temptations.*

---

[63]Matthew 6:21 (ESV).

*Pray for the people you know who believe they are one purchase away from happiness.*

**Further Reading in Scripture:**
- Matthew 6:19-21
- Matthew 6:25-34
- Matthew 16:26
- Luke 12:15
- 1 Timothy 6:9-10
- Hebrews 13:5

**Reflection:**
1. Consider everything the Lord has provided for you today; food, shelter, education, entertainment, friends, family, transportation, employment, mentors, etc. Are you grateful?
2. Discuss what you spend the majority of (or fantasize about spending) your money on? That will help you quickly identify where this idol has taken root.

**Further Readings:**
- Alcorn, Randy. *Managing God's Money: A Biblical Guide.* Carol Stream, IL: Tyndale, 2011.
- _____. *Money, Possessions, and Eternity: A Comprehensive Guide to What the* Bible *Says about Financial Stewardship, Generosity, Materialism, Retirement, Financial Planning, Gambling, Debt, and More.* Carol Stream, IL: Tyndale, 2021.
- DeMoss, Nancy. *Choosing Gratitude: Your Journey to Joy.* Chicago, IL: Moody, 2009.
- Evans, Tony. *Kingdom Stewardship.* Carol Stream, IL: Tyndale, 2020.

- Tripp, Paul David. *Redeeming Money: How God Reveals and Reorients Our Hearts*. Wheaton, IL: Crossway, 2018.
- _____. *Sex and Money: Pleasures That Leave You Empty and Grace that Satisfies*. Wheaton, IL: Crossway, 2013.

## The Idol of Control, Worry, and Fear

Before I begin this topic, I'd like to be clear that clinical anxiety and phobias are very real and should be managed by a Christian counselor in conjunction with a physician. This devotional is aimed at those who experience fear and worry rooted in the desire to be in ultimate control of everything -- like God (aka, this is for almost everyone). If you struggle with clinical anxiety, I highly encourage you to read *Finding Quiet* by Dr. J. P. Moreland. It has blessed many people greatly in their personal struggle with anxiety.

What is one of the dumbest bumper stickers of all time?

*Jesus is my co-pilot.*

Wrong.

Your life is completely in the hands of the pilot(s) when you fly. A better bumper sticker would be:

*I was dead -- Jesus brought me to life!*

There is something tremendously freeing in believing that *we are not in control*. Notice I said, believing, not knowing. Those are two very different things. You may have heard of God's "sovereignty," or his authority over all things, but do you *truly* believe God is in absolute control and directs everything for the good of those who love Him (Rom. 8:28)?

Two things destroy the idol of worry and control.

1. That I am fully accepted and loved by Jesus, the one who knows me best.
2. That Jesus is in complete control of my life.

The incarnation of Jesus is the most profound and beautiful fact I've ever encountered. It gives me deep, abiding hope. The one who knows me best, God, is the One who came after me. Let that wash over your soul. You need a friend, and there is no better friend than Jesus.

Remembering that I am fully accepted and loved by Jesus prevents those around me from controlling my mood. What they think, ultimately, does not matter. This is a common anxiety reduction technique, but instead of having to love and accept myself (which I will fail at), Jesus will remind me who I am and reminds me of His love. I meditate on passages like 2 Timothy 1:7-10: *for God gave us a spirit not of fear but of power and love and self-control.*

Remembering that Jesus is in complete control of my life eliminates my fears of the future or my own poor performance.

When our minds are like hamsters spinning in a wheel, we must shift our thoughts to the things of God.

*For every look at yourself, take 10 looks at Christ.*[64]

This is an exercise that the Spirit strengthens over time. I ask the Spirit to make my mind radically God-centered every day. As John Piper has said, *"...no one walks away from the Grand Canyon with a bigger view of himself."* No one gets too deep into their own mind if they are centered on the glory of God. This will not happen overnight. Sanctification is a process. I promise, if you are open with God and others, things will get better. Find a good doctor who will respect your Christian views. Please talk with a Christian counselor. Share your struggles with your pastor. God has placed them in your life for a reason. Above all, remember:

"My grace is sufficient for you," Jesus says,
"for my power is made perfect in weakness."[65]

You and I will not suffer with worry forever. One day, Jesus will tear open the heavens to return for His church. At that moment, we will become like Him. You and I will have incorruptible bodies, fully complete in the joyful presence of our Savior.

## Further Reading in Scripture:
- Matthew 6:25-34
- Romans 5:1

---

[64]M'Cheyne, Robert Murray.
[65]2 Corinthians 12:9 (ESV).

- Philippians 4:6
- 1 Peter 5:7

**Reflection:**

1. What do you constantly worry about?
2. What are you afraid of losing control over?
3. Meditate on the *further reading in Scripture* passages and discuss: could my desire to control everything be caused by a lack of faith in God's promises?

**Further Readings:**

- Fitzpatrick, Elyse. *Overcoming Fear, Worry, and Anxiety: Becoming a Woman of Faith and Confidence.* Eugene, OR: Harvest House Publishers, 2001.
- MacArthur, John. *Anxious for Nothing: God's Cure for the Cares of Your Soul.* Colorado Springs, CO: David C. Cook, 2012.
- _____. *Found: God's Peace: Experience True Freedom from Anxiety in Every Circumstance.* Colorado Springs, CO: David C. Cook, 2015.
- Moreland, J. P. *Finding Quiet: My Story of Overcoming Anxiety and the Practices that Brought Peace.* Grand Rapids, MI: Zondervan, 2019.
- Welch, Edward. *When I Am Afraid: A Step-by-Step Guide Away from Fear and Anxiety.* Greensboro, NC: New Growth Press, 2010.

# The Idol of Entertainment

There is a quote from the end of Francis Chan's book, *Crazy Love,* that I've never been able to get out of my head. He says, "I just don't know if this is where I want to be when Jesus returns. I'd rather be out helping someone or on my knees praying. I don't want Him to return and find me sitting in a theater."[66]

How much time do we spend in the theater of life? How much time do we spend escaping interactions with the very people God has put into our lives?

I do not believe leisure is inherently sinful. God commands us to rest on the Sabbath. The Lord rested on the seventh day of creation not because He needed to, but because we do. But rest becomes sloth when it dominates our time and motivations.

Entertainment is a dangerous idol because we become what we consume. Filling your mind with filth will produce filth in your life. We soothe our consciences with "the story is incredible," "it's a redemptive plot!" or "the show portrays violence accurately." You must ask yourself, *am I entertained by the sins Christ died for*? Am I enjoying the violence, sexual content, and perversion on the screen?

---

[66]Chan, Francis, *Crazy Love.*

Not only that, but entertainment can rob years from us. Our homes have more screens than people. And those screens are turned on for more than a third of the day--eight hours, 14 minutes.[67]

At the end of time, we will all give an account to Jesus of how we used his gifts (Matt 25:14-30). How many hours have we wasted? Time is a gift. Think of the countless seconds pointless things have occupied our minds. Do we really want to waste anymore? On the other side of eternity, no one will care about the shows we binge-watched or the sports we ordered our lives around.

**Further reading in Scripture:**
- Psalm 90:12
- Psalm 103:15-18
- Matthew 25:14-30
- Ephesians 5:15-17

**Reflection:**
1. How many hours a day do you spend on your phone or watching TV?
2. If you are a Christian, Jesus is redeeming every part of your life. He's redeeming your mind (changed thoughts), redeeming your desires (fleeing from sin quicker), and redeeming the world around you (through the church). Maybe it's time for you to realize He can redeem the hours of your day as well?

---

[67]USA Today.

3. How much time do you set aside to sit with God in prayer and in His Word?

4. How much time do you set aside to spend with others?

**Further Readings:**

- Detweiler, Craig. *iGods: How Technology Shapes Our Spiritual and Social Lives*. Grand Rapids, MI: Brazos Press, 2013.

- Kizer, Drew. *Dangerous Playground: The Christian and Social Media*. Leeds, AL: Riddle Creek Publishing, 2019.

- McCracken, Brett. *The Wisdom Pyramid: Feeding Your Soul in a Post-Truth World*. Wheaton, IL: Crossway, 2021.

- Reinke, Tony. *12 Ways Your Phone is Changing You*. Wheaton, IL: Crossway, 2017.

- _____. *Competing Spectacles: Treasuring Christ in the Media Age*. Wheaton, IL: Crossway, 2019.

# Smashing Idols

How can you take your sins to God? Because Jesus has already bore them. Christ has dealt with your sins. He died to free us from these idols we've identified together. Remember, idolatry is voluntary slavery. I pray Jesus has used this devotional to give you clarity **that leads to repentance and freedom**.

Name your sins, cry out to God, and ask Him to eliminate the idols. Ambiguous confession is useless. Get specific. God already knows! There is freedom in identifying the dark corners of your soul. Ask the Spirit to light them up and equip you to destroy the idols that enslave you. Otherwise, you will be trapped in an endless cycle of returning to the feet of the same idol.

> "Don't you realize that you become the slave of whatever you choose to obey? You can be a slave to sin, which leads to death, or you can choose to obey God, which leads to righteous living." [68]

> "For the Lord Himself will come down from heaven with a commanding shout, with the voice of the archangel, and with the trumpet call of God. First, the believers who have died will rise from their graves. Then, together with them, we

---

[68]Romans 6:16 (NLT).

who are still alive and remain on the earth will be caught up in the clouds to meet the Lord in the air. Then we will be with the Lord forever."[69]

Jesus is alive, and He is coming back. I join with Paul when he says of all who are reading this and have been born again,

"I am sure of this, that he who began a good work in you will bring it to completion at the day of Jesus Christ."[70]

Grace and peace be to you, my brothers and sisters.

**Further Readings:**
- Beale, G. K. *We Become What We Worship: A Biblical Theology of Idolatry*. Downers Grove, Ill.: InterVarsity Press, 2008.
- Keller, Timothy. *Counterfeit Gods: The Empty Promises of Money, Sex, and Power, and the Only Hope That Matters*. New York: Riverhead Books, 2011.
- Lane, Timothy, and Paul David Tripp. *How People Change*. Greensboro, NC: New Growth Press, 2006.
- Oden, Thomas C. "No Other Gods" in Carl Braaten, Christopher Seitz, eds., *I Am The Lord Your God: Christian Reflections on the Ten Commandments*. Grand Rapids, Mich.: Eerdmans, 2005.

---

[69]1 Thessalonians 4:16-17 (NLT).
[70]Philippians 1:6 (ESV).

- Ortlund, Dane. *Deeper: Real Change for Real Sinners.* Wheaton, IL: Crossway, 2021.

38048232R00059